Boloroo's BIG Question

Written by Michael Lacey Freeman

Illustrated by Baska Agul

BOLOROO'S BIG QUESTION

Independently Published by:
Michael Lacey Freeman, Italy
Email: michaellaceyfreeman@gmail.com
www.michaellaceyfreeman.com
© All rights reserved.

Published 2023
ISBN: 978-1-7394459-2-8

No part of this book may be reproduced, or stored in a retrieval system, or transmitted in any form or by any means, electronic, mechanical, photocopying, recording, or otherwise, without express written permission of the publisher.

Michael Lacey Freeman
Boloroo's BIG Question

Michael with some of his friends and colleagues from Lingors
(from left to right)
Gantsetseg Ganbaatar - Sumiya Dulamtsoo - Sainbileg Bayarkhuu
Nyamtaivan Odongeren - Michael Lacey Freeman
Tuvaansuren Savaandorj - Oyuntuya Munkhbaatar - Khurts Sanduijav
<u>Other team members</u>:
Bayartuya Byambasuren - Davaadorj Sumiyabazar - Temuujin Purevjav
Dulamsuren Erdenechimeg - Nyamdorj Sharavpurev

"I call your name behind my fears.
You make me strong today"

From the song: 'Butterfly'
(Paoloni/Lacey Freeman)

Contents

Page

6		Main Characters
8	Chapter 1	Questions! Questions! Questions!
13	Chapter 2	The Best Years of Your Life
17	Chapter 3	The Peach
24	Chapter 4	Buzz
29	Chapter 5	Telescopes and Microscopes
34	Chapter 6	The Red Carpet
42	Chapter 7	Boloroo's Big Answer
47	Chapter 8	New Questions
48		Happiness
50		Sing Along! Lyrics for: 'Butterfly'
52		About the Author
55		About the Illustrator
57		About Lingors
60		Test Your Memory
62		Bonus Story – 'What Happens Next?'
77		Test Your Memory Answers
79		Boloroo: The Next Adventure (Preview)
81		Stories by Michael Lacey Freeman

Main Characters

Chapter 1:

Questions !!! Questions!!! Questions!!!

Hello! Pleased to meet you. My name's Boloroo. I live in Italy, but my parents come from Mongolia. That is why I have this name. It's not a difficult name to say, 'Botro'. That's the way you say it.

I came to Italy when I was a little girl. One day I will go back to Mongolia. I want to see my Emee again. Emee means grandmother in Mongolian.

My Emee!!!

I still remember her songs and her stories before bedtime.

I would like to see her again soon, and to listen to more of her stories.

Mum says I'm like my grandmother because I never stop asking questions. I'm never satisfied. As soon as I get the answer to one question, I have another bigger question ready.

I remember one day, when I was very little, I asked my mother, 'Mum, what's the biggest number?'

'There is no biggest number,' said my mum. 'Numbers never end. They can go on forever.'

I was horrified by this. 'Numbers never end!' I thought. At that age I could count up to 100. That seemed like a very big number indeed. I was always very good at playing Hide and Seek, and I always wanted to be the person who counted and then looked for my friends.

I was always very good at playing 'Hide and Seek'.

I counted while my friends found a good hiding place.

'96, 97, 98, 99'

'100!'

'I'm coming to find you now,' I said.

I always found my friends very quickly. Teresa in the bathroom, Alice under the table, Filippo in the wardrobe, Letizia behind a tree. I loved playing that game.

So, when I found out that numbers never end, I was very angry indeed.

'Why do I need to learn numbers if they never end?' I asked my mother. 'I will never know them all!'

Mum laughed when she heard this. I was very angry with numbers for a while. But this didn't stop me from asking questions. And the questions changed as I got older.

'Why is the sky blue?'

'Why do we have to eat vegetables?'

'What are stars?'

'Does anyone live on the moon?'

'Can I have a pet?'

'Why do we have to go to sleep?'

And then when I started school the questions got more complicated.

'Where do babies come from?'

'Why do we have to go to school?'

'Where do we go when we die?'

'What are dreams?'

'How do plants grow?'

'How do airplanes fly?'

'Why do people have different skin colours?'

And then as I got even older, I started to look for answers to questions by myself. The Internet helped me to answer questions like these:

'What is gravity?'

'How does electricity work?'

'Why do zebras have stripes?

I also like to experiment in real life. And sometimes my experiments are quite silly.

One day I wanted to try to cook an egg on the street. I did it on a very hot day. I watched the egg sitting there, uncooked. And then I thought, 'Don't be silly Bolorco. Cooking an egg on the street makes no sense anyway, when there is a perfectly good frying pan at home.'

And once I wanted to teach my dog, Basar, to use the toilet. I soon discovered that dogs do not like using the toilet. They have to go to the toilet in their own way.

I even asked Basar questions because I liked the way he moved his head when I asked them. He wasn't able to answer my questions, but he looked so funny, and he really tried to understand me when I asked them.

Now I have a new dog.

Basar died last year, and it broke my heart. I still cry when I think of him. My new dog's name is Bankhar, and we spend a lot of time together.

I like asking questions more than answering them. I think my teachers get worried when I put my hand up in class.

This is why I love reading stories so much. When you read a story, there is always the most important question in the world that needs an answer.

WHAT HAPPENS NEXT?

Yes, I love questions. But there is one question that nobody can answer. I asked this question when Basar died and I don't know how to answer it.

I ask it every day. And the answer is always the same.

'I don't know!'

Chapter 2:
The Best Years of Your Life

There are two things that always make me feel sad.

1. When I think of Basar. I miss him so much.
2. When my dad goes away for work. He often has to be away from home for a long time when he works. He is a member of a film crew and sometimes, when he is making a movie, I don't see him for weeks and weeks and months and months.

Dad is not an actor or anything like that. He does things to help to make the film. He moves the cameras around, and the scenery, and he takes the actors to places they have to go to. When he makes a film, I ask if I can go with him. But he always says, 'Boloroo, you're too young and you can't miss school.'

When I'm older I will go with him. Or maybe I will become a movie star. Why not?

I miss dad a lot. Sure, we can chat on video, but it's not the same thing. A video can't give you a hug.

These moments of sadness make it even more important for me to find an answer to my big question.

Mum is the first person I ask my question to. It doesn't go well.

'Mum,'

'Yes,'

'Why do we have to be unhappy? Is there a way that we can be happy ALL the time?'

I need to know the answer to this question because I really want to be happy all of the time, or at least most of the time. Happiness is like a really delicious cake, and it's good to know what ingredients you need to make it.

'I don't know. It's something I don't think about, dear,' said mum. 'I have so many things to do, and there is no time to answer a question like this. I will have time when your dad comes back, and we can go on holiday. But right now, I just don't know.'

This answer doesn't satisfy me, so I ask her again.

'Can't you tell me? What are the ingredients of happiness? How can I be happy ALL the time?'

Mum stops for a second to think about it. She knows that when I have a question the best thing to do is to try and answer it.

'School,' says mum.

'What do you mean?' I say.

'School was the happiest time of my life. And it should be the happiest time of your life too.'

'But mum! I hope I'll have happier moments than school,' I say.

School makes me think of Madison who is always mean to me. She calls me Bookworm because I like books so much and she also calls me 'Science Nerd' when I put my hand up in class.

Mum stopped for a second to think about it.

Of course, there are good moments at school. I love History lessons because of my teacher, Mr. Davies. He makes everything feel like a really exciting story.

I like his lessons.

And I like other subjects like Art and Biology. I also love playing basketball and spending time with my best friend, Olivia. There are lots of things I like.

I do like school.

But I'm not happy ALL the time. Just some of the time.

'Is school the best it can be? I want to be happier than this,' I think.

'But, but' I say to my mum.

'No more ifs and buts right now,' says mum. 'It's time for you to go to school. If you're late for school, you won't be happy, and the teacher certainly won't be happy.'

So, I go to school that day with this question still on my mind.

'I will try to like school as much as possible,' I remember thinking. 'I need to try to like it all the time, and not just some of the time.'

Chapter 3:
The Peach

For days and days, and weeks, and weeks, I try to like school, but nothing changes. Sometimes it is good and sometimes it is not so good. There are good days and bad days, and it doesn't matter what I do, it is always like this.

One day when I am at school, I decide that I need to ask my big question to someone else.

'Mum can't possibly know everything. She doesn't know how to be happy ALL the time, but someone must know.'

'Who can I ask?'

Just at that moment, when I am thinking about these things, Mr. Davies walks into the classroom. It is time for History, my favourite subject.

'I will think about who I can ask after school,' I think.

Mr. Davies stands in front of the class and looks around the room. He puts his hands on his desk and smiles. And then he starts speaking. When he speaks, everyone listens. He is that kind of teacher. Everyone likes him.

'Good morning 3b! Today I'm going to tell you about the Second Industrial Revolution. Does anyone know anything about what the Second Industrial Revolution is?'

I think about it. I know there was a first industrial revolution, but I don't know anything about a second one.

There is silence in the class.

'Well, now I will show you something,' says Mr. Davies.

He moves to the back of the class, and everyone turns round to see what he is going to do.

'Are you ready? he says. Now, imagine life with no second industrial revolution,'

Mr. Davies switches off something and suddenly the computer makes a bleeping noise, the lights go out, the interactive whiteboard goes off.

'Ah, Electricity,' I say.

'Ah, Science Nerd,' says Madison.

'That's right Boloroo,' says Mr. Davies.

Mr. Davies always does things like this. He makes us think all the time by doing things and not just telling us things.

'And now, give me your mobile phones!'

'What??? Nooooo!!! says everyone in class 3b, including me.

'Ha-ha!' says Mr. Davies.

'Without the Second Industrial Revolution there is no electricity, there are no mobile phones. There is no Netflix, no profile pics, no light, and no going out when it gets dark.'

'Wow!' I think. 'A lot of the things I do today, things that are normal for me are because of scientists who lived a long time ago. They were people who asked questions and looked for answers. Their questions helped them to discover things and make things that are important to us. It's not so bad to ask questions, then.'

The lesson was amazing, and we learnt that people who asked interesting questions made motor cars, airplanes, telephones and a million other things.

'My question is also very interesting,' I thought. 'And I'm sure Mr. Davies can answer it. He will know the answer. He's the happiest person I know.'

The lesson ends and it is break-time. This is the perfect opportunity for me to ask my question. But I want to ask it when I am alone. I wait for Madison to eave the class and then I walk up to Mr. Davies' desk.

'Mr. Davies.'

'Ah, Boloroo! I imagine you have a question for me,' he says smiling.

'Yes, sir!' I say. 'But this one is really hard.'

Mr. Davies looks at me and smiles

'Well, let's see if I can answer it,' he says.

'It's not about History actually. It's more about life.'

'Ah life,' says Mr. Davies. 'Now that does sound interesting.'

'Well, I want to know about ... well, I was thinking about happiness.'

'Happiness?'

'Yes, I want to know what makes you so happy. Because I would like to be happy all the time, like you. And not just some of the time.'

'Oh, that is a big question,' says Mr. Davies.

'Yes, if you don't have time to answer, I will understand. You can think about it and let me know when you have the answer.'

'Mmmm, it's a very difficult question, but I'll try to answer it now,' says my teacher. 'You see, life is not simple. It's a bit like the rollercoasters you see when you go to the fun fair. Have you ever been on a rollercoaster?'

'Yes. I went on a rollercoaster once with Olivia. It was exciting but it made me feel a bit sick'

'Exactly! There are ups and downs. Good moments and bad moments. Moments when you are excited and happy and other moments when you feel a bit sick.'

'But you always seem so happy.'

'I try to be positive, especially when I'm in front of you students. And I love talking about History and that makes me happy. But sometimes I'm sad about things too. It's up and down really. Sometimes I'm happy but sometimes I'm sad.'

Then just for a moment Mr. Davies stops speaking. He is thinking. And then he says,

'You know something?'

'What, sir?' I answer.

'I think that the sad moments help us to enjoy the happy ones even more. We enjoy being happy because we know what it means to be sad.'

'I think I know what you mean,' I say.

'Think about a fish,' says Mr. Davies.

'A fish?'

'Yes, can a fish really understand how important water is until a fisherman takes it out of the water?'

'No, it can't,' says Mr. Davies answering his own question. 'A fish knows how important the water is only when it knows what it is like to be out of it.'

'So, you are saying that being sad helps us to understand what happiness is,' I say trying my best to understand. 'Being sad is like being a fish out of water. And being happy is like being in the water again.'

'The sad moments help us to enjoy the happy moments. Thank you, sir,' I say. 'I will think about what you said.'

'Keep asking questions, Boloroo. Just like the scientists of the Second Industrial Revolution. And keep looking for answers. The question you are asking is one of the greatest questions that we human beings can ask.'

'Thank you, Mr. Davies,' I say.

As I was leaving the room Mr. Davies says one more thing to me.

'Boloroo, please remember. If you study hard, you can do a job that you love doing, just like me. One way you can enjoy the rollercoaster of life more is to do something that you love doing.'

'I will remember this,' I say.

I smile at Mr. Davies. He is a kind man, and so clever!

I leave the classroom, but I don't go out into the playground. I am very hungry so I sit on a bench, take a peach out of my bag, and start to eat it.

'Mr. Davies has given me lots of things to think about,' I say to myself. 'He told me that my question is the greatest question we can ask,' I was very pleased with myself for asking this question. Even if I didn't get a clear answer.

I enjoy eating the peach. It is good. I love peaches. They are so sweet and tasty. As I am eating, I think about what job I would like to do in the future.

'Maybe a scientist, asking questions and discovering things', I think.

I take a bite from the peach, but it isn't so good anymore. In fact, it doesn't taste nice at all. I look at it. and see that there is a part of the peach that is black.

'Yuk!!!' I say.

And I put the peach in my bag and start to get ready for the next lesson.

But as I get up from the bench, I start to think about the peach again.

'Is this peach like life? When I first started eating it, it was good and then it was bad. Does this mean that the peach was a good peach or was it a bad peach?'

'Or both? Like the rollercoaster with its ups and downs.'

'Well now I have two hours of Maths,' I think.

'That is definitely like going down the rollercoaster!'

I look at it and see that there is a part of the peach that is black.

Chapter 4:
Buuz

Whenever I think of rollercoasters I always think of my best friend, Olivia. We went on a rollercoaster together last summer. Olivia's great. I can talk to her about everything, and we like the same things.

Every Thursday she comes to my house for dinner, and she always likes to try the things we eat.

On other days we normally eat Italian food at home but when Olivia is here it's a good excuse to eat stuff from Mongolia.

I don't remember much about living in Mongolia because I was so little when we came to live here, in Italy. But I love Mongolian food. It tastes like home. Last Thursday, Olivia tried a dish called, Buuz.

Peaches are sometimes good and sometimes bad, but Buuz is always delicious!

It was so funny listening to Olivia trying to say the word.

Buuz are fantastic to eat but difficult to pronounce.

'No, Olivia. Not buzz like a bee. It's not that kind of sound. It's not buzzzzzz.

'How do you say it then,' asked Olivia.

'It's a bit like Bot.'

'Bot,' said Olivia. But it still didn't sound right.

And we laughed so much.

Buuz are fantastic to eat but difficult to pronounce.

To eat Buuz properly you have to bite a little piece first. Then you drink the juice inside. After that you can eat the rest.

At first, she thought that Buuz were ravioli, which everyone eats in Italy. They look like ravioli, but they are different. Buuz have meat and onions in them, ravioli usually has cheese and spinach.

I go to Olivia's house on Fridays, and we always have pizza and watch a movie. I like going to her house because it's very noisy. There are always lots of things happening because Olivia has two little brothers, and with her mum and dad there too it's a fun place to be.

I like it. Sometimes it feels so lonely and quiet at my house with just me and mum. When dad isn't there, the whole house feels so empty.

It always makes me sad to think about these things and I talk to Olivia about them all the time. One Friday, just before we start watching a movie, I decide to ask her my big question.

'Maybe she has the answer,' I think.

And so, I ask.

'Olivia, do you think that I'm a happy person, most of the time?'

'Yes, you're very happy and always smiling, even when Madison says something bad about you, you don't feel down about it for very long.'

'Thank you. But sometimes I'm sad. I miss Basar and I hate it when Dad goes away for work. I like Davide in 4b, but he never even looks at me. That makes me sad too. What can I do about this? Do you think that there is any way to be happy all the time, and not be sad, ever?'

'I don't know. I sometimes feel down too. But I know one thing.'

'What?'

'It's my birthday in September and I'm going to get a new bike. When I get that I'll be able to go anywhere, anytime I want. I'll be able to come to your house and won't need mum or dad to drive me. I won't let my brothers touch it. I'll keep it in good condition. And I'll use it all the time. When I get my bike, then I'll be happy.'

'Yeah,' I said. 'That's right.'

I didn't tell Olivia what I really think. She is my best friend after all, and I don't want to hurt her feelings. But I don't think that a bike will make her happy all the time. I got a bike for my birthday last year, and I was so excited at first.

I still remember when I first saw it. It was red and green, and it had a beautiful basket on the front. It was shiny and new, and I imagined having all kinds of adventures on it. I even gave the bicycle a name, Sally!

On that day every five minutes I went to my bedroom window to look out into the garden. There it was! My bicycle! I looked at it and said,

'Sally! You are mine!'

On the first night, I even looked out of the window to say goodnight to Sally. And I asked mum to bring Sally into the house while I was sleeping because I was worried that a thief might take her away into the night.

But now I never think about my bike. I never go to the window to say goodnight to it, and I never ask for it to be in the house. I don't call it Sally anymore. It's in the garden shed, a bit dirty and forgotten. Will Olivia's bike be like that after a few months? Dirty and forgotten?

'If a thief takes my bike now, I won't be sad,' I say to myself. On Saturday it will be my birthday again. I don't know what present I am going to get. It's a special birthday. I will be 16 years old. I really would like a microscope. But now I know that a microscope isn't going to make me happy forever.

Chapter 5:

Telescopes and Microscopes

On Saturday, I woke up and stretched my arms out. I could see the light coming in from the window. It was a new day, a different day, a special day!

It was my birthday!

I washed and got dressed quickly. I could hear some noises in the living room already. Who was in the house? Was dad back home????

I didn't want to miss a single thing. When I was ready, I walked quietly along the corridor and stood by the door of the living room. Before going into the room, I listened.

'Sshhhhh! don't talk about the surprise party. Boloroo might hear you,' said one voice.

'She won't hear anything, don't worry. She always gets up late on a Saturday.' said the other.

The second voice was my mum. But I didn't recognise the first voice. It was probably a friend of my mum, a neighbour perhaps.

'A surprise party,' I thought.

'For me??'

'Per Moi??'

I said this in French too because I am learning French at school now.

'Sshhhhh! don't talk about the surprise party'

I stood in the corridor for a moment and whispered the words 'Oh wow!' about a thousand times.

Then the questions started to come really quickly.

'Why am I having a surprise party now?

Who will be coming?

Where will the party be?

Will the party be at home or in another place?

When will it begin?

How long will it last?

I couldn't answer these questions of course. That's why a surprise party is called a surprise party. Quietly I went back to my bedroom and waited for another fifteen minutes before coming out again. I didn't want mum to know what I knew.

When I went into the living room my mum was there, but there wasn't anyone else. Mum gave me my present. It was just what I wanted. A microscope.

I really need a microscope because it can help you to see the small things that you normally cannot see.

I was so excited about this. Somehow having a microscope seemed more exciting than having a telescope. Smaller things are more important than bigger things. The world of the big, the sky, the planets, the stars are all made of small things. We are made of small things. Everything is made of the small.

'I won't tell Madison about this present,' I thought. She'll call me a science nerd again. Ha-ha!

A microscope and a telescope can help you to answer many questions. But these things cannot answer my big question. That still needed an answer.

'Will I ever find the answer?' I asked myself.

Well, I didn't know it, but I was going to have another chance to ask my big question at my surprise party later that evening.

A microscope and a telescope can help you to answer many questions.

Chapter 6:

The Red Carpet

I am happy about having a surprise birthday party. And I think about it all day. I practise looking surprised.

'Ohhhh, I can't believe it', I say in front of the mirror. And then I put my hand to my mouth.

I think I'm a really good actor. That's why I think that I can become an actor and work with dad when he helps to make a movie.

All day, I keep practising walking into a room and looking surprised. I try to make myself cry a little bit. But I can only do that if I think of Basar.

The day goes really slowly. After breakfast mum tells me that we are going to my favourite restaurant, just me and her, to celebrate my birthday.

'Ha! Just me and her!' I think and smile.

I count the hours.

8 hours to go. I'm happy that I don't have to count up to 100,000,000 before my party begins.

7 hours to go. I read all the instructions for my microscope.

6 hours to go. I phone Olivia to see if she will tell me anything about the party. She doesn't tell me anything!

5 hours to go. I eat some crackers, but I'm not very hungry.

4 hours to go. The phone rings! It's dad!

'Hi Boloroo! My lovely girl! Happy Birthday!!!! I'm so sad that I can't be there today. I miss you so much. I'll see you very soon I promise.'

'That's okay, dad,' I said. 'I really miss you too. When are you coming back?'

'Soon Boloroo. As soon as we finish this movie. It won't be long.'

'And then you'll be at home, with me and mum for a long time, you promise?'

'Yes, I promise, my angel. Oh, by the way. Mum told me about your question. About happiness.'

'Yeah!'

'Do you want to know what I think?'

'Yeah! Of course, I do. I say.

'Well, I think that you can find happiness in the wings of a butterfly,' says dad.

'What does that mean?'

'I'll tell you soon, dear. I'll leave it for you to think about. You're so clever. You'll understand. I hope you like your microscope. Happy birthday again and see you very soon. Bye dear.'

'Bye dad!'

I'm happy and sad now . I'm happy to speak to dad, and to see his face on video. But that means that he isn't coming to my surprise birthday party. How much longer do I have to wait for my birthday party? Three and a half hours!!!!

I find some dust in my room and start to examine it with my microscope.

2 hours to go. I get washed and start to choose my clothes. I open my wardrobe and choose two of my favourite dresses. Which one shall I wear?

1 hour to go. I spend some time on my phone, but I am not concentrating on what I'm looking at.

Then I hear a car. My mum calls me. I run down and get into the car with mum. And we drive to the restaurant.

When we get out of the car I walk towards the restaurant and say to myself.

'Boloroo, remember to put on your surprised face as you walk in the room. Remember to say, Oh Wow, and to smile and to look excited, don't think of Basar, don't look for dad because he might not be there and …'

I was so worried about remembering all these things that I didn't even notice that a door was opening and then …

'Oh my!' I shouted.

Even if it wasn't really a surprise, it really did feel like a surprise at that moment.

The party was like the good part of the peach, the exciting part of the roller coaster.

Everyone in the room is filming the moment when I walk in. I feel like a film star walking along a red carpet.

Olivia and other friends from school are there. There are friends from my basketball team too and lots of mums and dads.

Even Bankhar is there waiting to say hello to me. Everybody is there in that room for me. They are all looking at me.

It is amazing!

People come up to speak to me and I hug them. There is music and Mongolian food and balloons and lots and lots of noise.

It's the best non-surprise surprise party that anyone could ever have!

And then after hugging about 100 people I see someone in the corner of the room.

This really is the biggest surprise ever!

In the corner of the room there is a little old lady with lots of lines on her face, and questions in her eyes. A wise old lady. A lady who knows about ups and downs and crying and laughing. A lady who knows about good peaches and bad peaches, and about being happy and sad.

It's Emee.

It is my grandma!!!

'Emee. You're here with me! I can't believe it. Oh my! Emee!

'My little Boloroo. So long. You were only five years old … the last time I saw you.'

'Emee,' was all I could say because I was crying.

Crying with happiness.

I feel like a film star walking along a red carpet.

I hold her. We hug. Everything else stops. I no longer hear the music in the room and the people speaking. It's just me and Emee and the roller coaster is going up and down at the same time as I smile and cry.

'Now this is what I call a surprise party', I say to myself.

I didn't want the party to end, ever! There are lots of yummy sandwiches, cakes, and biscuits, but I am not hungry and don't eat anything. I move from one person to the next and talk to everyone and then I keep going back to speak to my grandma because I cannot believe she is really there.

I just want nobody to leave ever and for the party to go on forever and forever.

But of course, there is nothing that lasts forever. Is there? Here I go again, asking questions. But everyone I love is in that room

Everyone I love apart from Dad and Basar, of course.

And then, once again when I think of this, I start to feel sad again.

How I miss them!

When the party finishes and we go home, I sit with my grandmother while my mother prepares the bedroom for her.

'Did you like the party, Boloroo? she asks.'

'Oh yes, Emee, I did. But I wanted dad to be there, and Basar too.'

'Yes, or course. I know your dad did everything he could to get back in time. I'm sure he'll be back soon.'

'Yes, I know Emee. Can I ask you something?'

'Yes, of course you can,' said Grandma.

'Why is it that so often I feel sad? Why can't I be happy, like I was at my party, most of the time and not just some of the time?'

My grandmother looked up at me and thought about my question. She sat there, silent for a while, and then she said.

'That's a difficult question my dear Boloroo. I don't know what to say. But, I can say this. I am sorry to hear that sometimes you feel sad. When I was young like you, I sometimes felt sad too, but most of my memories are happy ones. Now, as I get older there are more moments that are sadder. Many of my friends are no longer with me, and my body gets tired more quickly and I have so many aches, not just headaches and toothaches, but my body aches all over nearly all the time.'

'But then, now that I think about it, you can't have everything. It's better having some happy moments than not having any at all, and the longer I live, the more moments of happiness I will have.'

'Your grandfather always made me happy. He was a real gentleman and looked after me and made me feel special. When he died, things became more difficult for me. But I have you and your mum here in Italy and my brother and his children in Ulaanbaatar. I have this to be thankful for. We must be grateful Boloroo for all the good things in life. That's the closest we can get to happiness.'

Emee spoke a lot, but did she answer my question? I don't think so.

She talked about happness like it was a thing that belonged to the past and not the future. I understand this. My grandmother's past is much bigger than her future. No microscope or telescope can tell me how long my grandmother's future will be, but I know that this might be the last time I see her. And this was another sad thought.

Up and down. Up and down, we go.

'Well Emee. We are going to have a nice time together, now that you are here. I can show you around town, take you to the best cake shop in the world. We can take Bankhar with us to the park. You can meet my friend Olivia. I can show you how well I can swim. We can go to the zoo. There is a good one near here. We are going to have a really good time.'

And I was right.

We did have a great time.

Across the generations and across the skies, grandmother, mother, and daughter together for a brief but special moment in time.

It was good and maybe life doesn't get much better than this.

All the time there was a little thought in my head that I couldn't send away.

'Dad! Where are you?'

But as my grandmother said,

'We can't have everything.'

Chapter 7:

Boloroo's Big Answer

Grandmother left last weekend.

We said goodbye to her at the airport and I promised to phone her every week and to come to Mongolia as soon as possible.

It was fun to be with her. We did so many things together.

We went to the zoo. We went to the seaside. It wasn't a very warm day, but we all had an ice cream, and walked along the beach. We did some shopping at the mall and in the centre. We went to the cinema and saw a film, but I had to translate everything for her because she doesn't speak Italian. We had cups of tea and coffee wherever we went. And I even took Grandma to my school, but we didn't go inside together because I didn't want her to see Madison.

But most of the time we didn't go anywhere in particular. We talked and she told me stories about her life and about Mongolia. When I'm 18, I'll go back there to see what it's like. That's only two years from now. And then I will get to see other people in my family, my uncle, and my cousins.

But for now, my connection to Mongolia, my Emee is gone.

I sit in the park all alone, feeling a little sad, and no nearer to getting an answer to my question.

Well, I am not completely alone.

I am with Bankhar. He is sitting next to me. And so, I look into his eyes, and I ask him.

'Bankhar, how can I stop myself from being so unhappy? You always look so happy all the time, just like your brother dog, Basar. What's your secret?'

Bankhar moves his head to the right, just like Basar did. But of course, no answer comes.

'Ha-ha!' I say. 'Sorry Bankhar! I know that you can't tell me.'

And then I throw a big stick in the air and watch him chase it. I can let Bankhar run where he wants. He's a good dog, almost as good as Basar and I'm training him well. He doesn't go too far, and he always comes back when I call him.

As for an answer to my big question.

I asked my mum and dad, my teacher, my grandmother, my best friend. And now, even my dog.

But where is my dog?' I ask myself.

'Bankhar! Bankhar!'

Ah there he is. Going crazy. Sniffing the grass and the flowers and moving his tail. He looks so happy. Just being there in this moment, smelling all the smells and hearing all the sounds. He is so, so, so happy. I hope he doesn't disturb the butterflies.

'Bankhar!'

'Bankhar!'

'Oh Bankhar!'

And then, something happens.

Suddenly, I know.

'That's it!' I say to myself.

'Bankhar! Thank you! Thank you for answering my question!!!'

'Bankhar is answering it right now. Happiness is now. It is right there in the moment. It's in the air and on the flowers, it's in the sky and on the ground. It's everywhere! And there is Bankhar teaching me this right now.'

And then I think of all the special moments in my life. Eating a peach, and watching a film with Olivia, riding my bicycle, and sharing an ice cream with my grandma. Laughing at how Olivia says buzz, and opening my birthday presents. Walking into the restaurant like a movie star. Sitting by the fire and listening to grandma telling us stories. Being with mum and grandma, three girls together. All those moments. I was so busy thinking about how to be happy that I forgot

TO BE happy.

I forgot to be happy here and now and in the moment.

I forgot to smell the grass and the flowers, just like Bankhar.

Now!!! It's now!!!

I look at Bankhar. He is doing his crazy things. He is in love with this moment. I am going to hug him and hold him now.

'Bankhar!' I shout.

But Bankhar doesn't run to me.

'Bankhar! What are you doing now? Why are you running away from me?'

'Bankhar! Bankhar! Bankhar!'

Then I hear a voice.

Bankhar is answering it right now. Happiness is now.

Someone else is calling him. Bankhar is moving really fast across the field. I follow him with my eyes. And look at the direction he is running in.

And then I see a man, moving towards us.

At first, I don't understand who the man is. But as he gets nearer, I realise. It isn't just any man.

It's dad! He's home. He is here because he is looking for me.

'Dad!!!!' I shout.

And like Bankhar now I start to run, to run to my dad, knowing that he is going to hold me, and I want to enjoy every tiny little, microscopic microsecond of this moment, here and now. To enjoy the way he holds me, to listen to his voice, to enjoy it just like it is and be

Happy Now

Does my Big Question have an answer?

Well, it does for me. It has an answer now.

'Boloroo!!!' says dad. 'I got home, and your mum told me you were at the park. So, I came to find you.'

'I'm so happy you are here, dad,' I say.

'Me too, dear.'

'And I know what you mean about the butterflies,' I say, smiling.

'I'm sure you do,' says dad.

I walk home with dad and Bankhar. I went to the park alone, but I leave the park with everything I need to make me happy.

Chapter 8:

New Questions

How much water do people use every day?

Are there peaches in Mongolia?

What's the most powerful microscope in the world?

What do you have to do to become a history teacher?

Has there been a third industrial revolution?

Do dogs have feelings like us?

I'm sitting in my bedroom, now. Soon it will be dinner time. Mum and dad are downstairs. I am sure they have lots of things to talk about. I can smell dinner. It will be good.

I wish you were here to enjoy it with me.

Maybe next time!

I don't know what my next question will be. Asking questions is fun. You never know what will be around the corner. And that is what makes life fun.

But today I have learnt a big lesson.

And it was Bankhar who was my teacher.

You can learn from Bankhar too.

Smell the grass!

Be here! Now!

And never stop asking questions.

Happiness:

1. Here are some quotes from famous people about happiness. Which ones do you agree with most? Which ones are similar to your way of seeing life?

"Happiness is a direction not a place."

Sydney J Harris (Journalist)

"When you focus on the good, the good gets better".

Esther Hicks (Writer)

"The only thing that will make you happy is being happy with who you are".

Goldie Hawn (Actress)

"Happiness is a place between too much and too little"

Finnish Proverb

"Happiness is the best makeup".

Drew Barrymore (Actress).

"Simplicity makes me happy".

Alicia Keys (Singer)

"To fall in love with yourself is the first secret to happiness."

Robert Morley (Actor)

"If you want to live a happy life, tie it to a goal, not to people or things."

Albert Einstein (Scientist)

"If you see someone without a smile, give them one of yours".

Dolly Parton (Singer)

"Happiness is a state of mind. It's just according to the way you look at things".

Walt Disney (Film maker)

"Happiness is the secret to all beauty. There is no beauty without happiness".

Christian Dior (Stylist)

"There is no path to happiness. Happiness is the path".

Buddha

2. What is your philosophy?

Sing Along!
'Butterfly'
(Paoloni/Lacey Freeman)

You call my name with a word of whisper.

You've stolen my time.

And every season send my troubles.

To love that's close to my heart.

And the promise I can make today.

I'll remember to say keep my heart in its shape.

But now you were my butterfly.

You were the cure of my life.

In the silent night embrace me again.

But it's real, it's real.

I call your name behind my fears.

You make me strong today.

Between our days I'll clear all signs.

Of time inside my heart.

And the promise I can make today.

I'll remember to say keep my heart in its shape.

But now you were my butterfly.

You were the cure of my life.

Fly away my lovely.
And leave my side.
Fly away my sweetheart.
And let me die.

And the promise I can make today.
I'll remember to say.
Keep my heart in its shape.

But now you were my butterfly.
You were the cure of my life.
In the silent night embrace me again
But it's real, it's real.

You were my butterfly.

You were my butterfly.

You were my butterfly.

(You can find this song on Michael's YouTube channel)

About the Author

Hello! My name is Michael Lacey Freeman, and I am the writer of this story. I come from a town called Rochford, near London in the UK but I live in Italy now with my family.

I have always loved reading stories and now I feel lucky that I have the opportunity to actually write stories too. I share my stories with people from all over the world and have recently been to Indonesia, Vietnam and Mongolia to spread the message that words are powerful. I have told my stories to many people online too.

I also love music and make songs with my band, *The Eggheads*. We make songs for the stories I write and the song for this story is called, *Butterfly*.

The Stories

Perhaps my most popular story is *Egghead*. It is a story about a little boy who is bullied at school. It is a true story. I should know that it is true because the little boy in the story was me. Recently I have written a sequel to this story, called *Egghead the Movie*. I have written other stories like *Dot to Dot, All the Colours of Sam* and *The Drum* and of course *Boloroo's Big Question*.

Boloroo's Big Question

I enjoyed writing Boloroo's Big Question. I love Boloroo because she is a curious girl. She always asks questions, and she is always positive. I hope to write many more stories in the future about her. I also love Boloroo because of the connection she has with Mongolia, a fascinating and beautiful country.

I hope you enjoyed reading about Boloroo as much as I enjoyed writing about her.

Questions

It's always important to ask questions. Asking questions is one of the things that unites us. It makes us human. For me, the most important question in the world is, what happens next? I hope that you continue reading stories and finding answers to this wonderful question.

Michael with Oyuntuya Munkhbaatar and Sumiya Dulamtsoo and Boloroo at the Extensive Reading World Congress in Denpasar, Indonesia in August 2023

Michael Lacey Freeman

About the Illustrator

The Early Years

Hello! My name is Baasankhuu Tsogtbaatar, I am a designer and illustration artist. My artist's name is Baska Agul.

I was born in Mongolia. When I was a child, I spent my summer holidays at my grandmother's house in the country. That time of my life was great for two reasons. Firstly, I had time to play with my cousins. Secondly, when you go outside the city you can find great places to go swimming and ride horses. There are also many other animals like cows and sheep.

My Work and Studies

I studied in a small school outside the city, and from the beginning I was interested in drawing. That is why after my first school I went to a design school to become a graphic designer.

I will always have this passion for art and drawing and I was so happy to work on the Boloroo project.

I also worked on the illustrations for another project called, 'The Big Crystal Question Book'. It is amazing to know that people from many countries will see my drawings. It is great fun to try to draw pictures that will help children to understand the text.

Boloroo's Big Question

I am very happy to learn many things, not just about drawing, like exploring my imagination. Thanks to author Michael for the opportunity to collaborate on this book.

I hope we will work together again in the future. I would like to thank my friends and family for always supporting my passion for painting.

I hope you like my work. If interested, you can find out more about what I do on Instagram.

Instagram: baska_agul

Over to You

What do you think? What is your favourite illustration in this story?

Baska Agul

About Lingors (Mongolia)

Lingors is an educational iinstitute. We are famous for creating our first ever Reading Marathon in Mongolia. In the marathon everyone can read at their own pace while sharing news of their reading adventure to fellow readers during the competition. There are several different types of marathons. One of them is called a 'team marathor' There are also individual marathons.

While children and adults read books in English, they read a lot of different books. One of them was 'Egghead' by Michael Lacey Freeman. Marathon readers, especially kids, really loved this wonderful story so the Lingors team decided to organize an author's meeting where kids could meet the actual real-life Egghead (Michael) online. The meeting was a huge success!!! Kids wanted to meet the author in person so Lingors invited him from Italy to come and visit Mongolia.

We crossed paths with the fantastic Michael Lacey Freeman in 2021 during the Extensive Reading Foundation World Congress, and since then, we've been teaming up on various exciting projects.

One of our proudest collaborations is the 'Meet the Author' series, featuring the talented Michael Lacey Freeman. As a result of these meetings, we decided to put his most famous 21 stories from his life experience in our special Marathon called 'Journey with Michael'. You can read his other stories in the series on the Lingors app.

Michael was so impressed with the dedication of Mongolian students that he decided to write a special story about a delightful Mongolian girl named Boloroo, endtitled 'Boloroo's Big Question.'

The Reading Marathon

This is just the beginning – we're thrilled to share that more enchanting tales by Michael Lacey Freeman are in the pipeline for the future. Stay tuned for more literary magic!

Test Your Memory

1. What does Boloroo call her grandmother?

2. How do you pronounce the name Boloroo?

3. What is Boloroo's favourite question?

4. What years are the happiest according to Boloroo's mum?

5. What was Boloroo's history lesson about?

6. What snack did Boloroo eat after the history lesson?

7. What Mongolian meal did Olivia eat at Boloroo's house?

8. Why does Boloroo like going to Olivia's house?

9. What did Boloroo want for her birthday and why did she want it?

10. How did Boloroo know about the surprise party?

11 Who is Madison?

12 What is Boloroo's dad's answer to the big question?

13 What does Boloroo examine with her birthday present?

14 What is the biggest surprise for Boloroo at her birthday party?

15 Who lives in Mongolia with Boloroo's grandmother?

16 Name three places that Boloroo goes to with her grandmother.

17 Where does Bolorco see her dad again?

18 What did Boloroo's dad mean when he talked about happiness being on the wings of a butterfly?

19 Name two questions that Boloroo asks in the last chapter.

20 Do some research and answer the two questions you have chosen when you answered question 19.

BONUS STORY

What Happens Next?

By Michael Lacey Freeman

Chapter 1 - Poor Mr. Twiddle!

When I was a child, my favourite book was '*The Stories of Mr. Twiddle.*' I don't know how many times I read the stories inside that book, night after night. Whatever happened during the day, even if it was really bad, I always knew that in the evening Mr. Twiddle would help me. He would keep me company and make me feel better.

I still have the book. And I still have the memories.

As I'm sure you can imagine, Mr. Twiddle was the main character of these stories. He is a nice old man who never has a bad word to say about anyone. He is the kind of man who says good morning to everyone he meets, who whistles on his way to work, who stops to stroke a dog or smile at a baby, and who is always ready to say something nice about you.

'Hey Cherub! How are you today? I like your bicycle. Is it new?'

He is the kind of person who makes you feel very special because he has all the time in the world to listen to you.

I am sure that everyone has a Mr. Twiddle in their life. I hope that there are lots of Mr and Mrs. Twiddles in every country and in every town in the world.

Do you have one?

My Mr. Twiddle only has one problem. And this problem is the reason that he has so many memorable adventures and gets into so many difficulties.

He is very forgetful. He forgets everything! He goes out in the rain and forgets his umbrella. He leaves the house and forgets to turn things off, like the lights and the oven, but also forgets to turn things on like the heating and the security system. He can never find anything he loses because he is always losing his glasses. He finds himself looking for his hat and forgets that it is on his head.

Many children around the world loved reading about him. And I was one of those children. Mr. Twiddle never remembers anything, and that is why children will never forget him.

Poor Mr. Twiddle! I say to myself as I look at the book again and remember what a great friend he was to me when I was a child. But he wasn't just a friend of my mine. He was also a friend of Alice, my daughter.

I open the book now and it reminds me of the days I told these wonderful stories to her, when she was only five years old.

Alice loved those stories as much as I did. She would lay there in bed, wide-eyed, taking in every detail just like me, living inside those stories, hiding under the sheets when Mr. Twiddle was in danger – and smiling when he was victorious.

Chapter 2 - Running for No Reason

Alice and I love Mr. Twiddle!

I remember when I held my Alice in my arms for the first time. She looked like a mini version of me (much better looking of course). She had just arrived in the world. She was brand new! And when I looked at her face for the first time, my world changed in one instant.

'Michael,' I said to myself. 'This is something for life. It is forever. You have a big responsibility now. You have to teach your daughter how to be happy and confident. You have to make sure she has a good start in life. You must be her teacher, and you cannot make any mistakes.'

The words that I said to myself that day frightened me. How could I look after a little baby like this? I had never done such a thing before in my life. Would I be any good at it? I wasn't very good at looking after myself. How could I look after this beautiful baby, my daughter? What if I make a mistake? What do you do? Where are the books? Who can help me? What do I need to know? How can I be her teacher?

These were the questions on my mind, on that day.

Of course, on that day I didn't know that I would learn all I needed to know, as all parents do. I didn't know that I had the one thing, and maybe the only thing that anyone needs.

That thing was love.

But on that day, when complete joy and complete terror lived side by side in my head, there was something else that I didn't know.

I didn't know that Alice would not just be my student, but she was also going to be my teacher. Yes, I taught Alice many things, but she taught me more. She helped me to remember what it was like to be a child myself. Often as we grow, we forget so many things about life. Alice helped me to remember these things.

Let me give you an example of this. One day, Alice taught me to run for no reason.

I love the mornings and I like to get up when most other people are sleeping. My wife liked this habit of mine when Alice was born because when Alice woke up at 5am I was happy to take her downstairs to play with her.

At first, Alice was happy just to play with my house keys, but when she started to walk, the games she wanted to play became more and more sophisticated. She wanted to be Sleeping Beauty, Cinderella, and Snow White, and I would have to be all the other characters. I would read stories to her every day and invent stories of my own for her too.

One day when we came downstairs, Alice saw a toy that she really wanted to play with. It was only a few metres away, but she ran towards it as quickly as she could. I watched her do this and thought to myself.

'When is the last time I ever ran like that? I always run for a reason, if I am late for a bus, a train, or an appointment. But when did I ever run to pick up a book or to turn the radio on?'

The answer was never. I just didn't. I never ran for no reason.

But now that I thought of it, Alice did this all the time, as most children do.

So, I decided to try it for myself.

The next morning, we came downstairs. And I ran to the fridge. Only for a few metres. And you know what?

It felt really good!

Children never do anything for no reason. Running for no reason gives you energy. When I run like that it gives me a bigger energy boost than the coffee I drink afterwards.

So, what are you waiting for?

Tomorrow

Remember!

Run for no reason.

And see what happens.

Chapter 3 - The Breeze!

Would you like another example of how Alice was my teacher?

I remember one time in the summer, when Alice and I were in our garden. It was a beautiful summer day, but I hadn't really noticed this. I had so much homework to correct and I had lessons to plan for the next day. So, I sat with Alice and worked while she played with something.

But Alice was not happy with this at all.

'Daddy,' she said. 'Daddy!'.

I put my book down. 'What is it, Alice?'

I looked at her as I asked this question. She was smiling, and both her arms were stretched out, up towards the sky.

'The breeze,' she said. 'Feel the breeze.'

I lifted my arms in the air, just like her and felt the breeze, the soft, sweet wind, caressing my arms.

It felt special. Father and daughter holding their arms out to greet a welcoming sky.

It is something that is there all the time. But I hadn't noticed it. I was so busy thinking about what I had to do tomorrow, that I forgot about today.

But Alice helped me to remember, and this is why every day, even if I am really busy, I always find some time to feel the breeze.

And when I feel it, I close my eyes and feel God's whisper. So, what are you waiting for? Take some time each day to feel the breeze.

Chapter 4 - Mr. Twiddle Comes to the Rescue!

I learnt about the breeze in the summer but Alice taught me the most important lesson of all in the winter.

One afternoon, during the winter of 2004, Alice, my wife, and I were sitting in the living room, watching TV.

Alice wasn't playing or running or smiling at this particular time. She couldn't do these things because she wasn't feeling well. She had a bad cold.

Nothing strange about that you might say. Children have colds all the time. But this was a strange cold because it didn't seem to go away.

My wife and I waited for a few days to see if it would pass. But it seemed to be getting worse and not better.

And by late evening Alice began to have difficulty breathing.

My wife Paola, and I looked at each other. We were so worried. But without even speaking we knew what we had to do.

We got in the car and my wife started to drive towards the local hospital. I sat in the back of the car with Alice because somehow, I knew what I had to do at the moment.

In the car, Alice was frightened. 'I can't ... I can't breathe daddy. Where are we going?' she asked. She looked around. What was normally familiar to her was strange and frightening at that moment. I had decided to sit with her in the back of the car for one important reason.

I knew that I had to tell her a story. It was always what we did together. It was the most familiar thing I could think of. I always told her stories. Daytime, night time, anytime. But I didn't know what story to tell. And then I had an idea.

'Mr. Twiddle will help me.'

Chapter 5 - A New Story

I didn't have the book with me, so I had to invent a new Mr. Twiddle story.

One morning Mr. Twiddle woke up late. 'I'm late, so late,' he said. 'I've got to get to work. I've got to catch the bus.

Quick! Quick!'

Mr. Twiddle ran out of the house. But he forgot one important thing. He forgot to get dressed, and was still in his pyjamas.

It was working.

I had Alice's attention. She was still in pain. She was still confused. But her big brown eyes were fixed on mine. I didn't hesitate, and continued with the story.

On his way to the bus stop he passed Mrs. Wright, his neighbour. 'Mr. Twiddle, Mr. Twiddle!' she shouted.

'Good morning, Mrs. Wright. Good morning. Sorry I can't stop, I'm so late. Oh no, what will my boss say?'

'But Mr. Twiddle! Mr. Twiddle!'

Alice was still finding it difficult to breathe, but she wasn't crying any more. She was inside the story. She was watching Mr. Twiddle fighting the wind and rain, making his way to the bus stop.

Mr. Twiddle arrived at the bus stop. Luckily at that moment, the number 8 bus turned into the road, where Mr. Twiddle was waiting. 'Oh, thank goodness!' thought Mr. Twiddle. I'm so lucky. The number 8 bus takes me just outside my office.'

We were getting near the hospital. I was holding Alice's head in my arms. Alice was with me but by now she was also somewhere else.

She was on the bus with Mr. Twiddle.

Mr. Twiddle got on the bus. 'Ah there's a seat,' he said to himself. 'May I sit next to you,' asked Mr. Twiddle to the person sitting by the window. The woman looked at Mr. Twiddle and said,

'No, wait. I ...I'm getting, getting off at the next stop.'

'What luck!' thought Mr. Twiddle. 'A seat by the window.'

He sat and looked out of the window. The people he saw on the pavement looked at him in a strange way. But he didn't know why. Then he heard a little voice. It was the voice of a little boy.

'Look Mummy, look!' the little boy said. 'That man's still got his pyjamas on.' Mr. Twiddle looked at himself. 'Oh my!' he said.

And after saying those words, everybody on the bus started laughing.

'Oh Mr. Twiddle! What will you do next' said a young girl sitting behind him.

'Here we are!' said my wife.

I stopped telling the story and looked out of the car window. We were there. We were at the hospital.

'Yes, here we are,' I said to Alice, and I picked her up so that I could carry her into the hospital.

'Now, I'm going to take you to see a nice lady. And she is going to make you better.' I said.

'Daddy! Daddy!' cried Alice.

'What Alice, What?' I cried back. I was frightened and was not doing a very good job of hiding it.

And then she gave me my greatest lesson. Do you know what it was?

Chapter 6 - Dust

'WHAT HA- HAPPENS NEXT?' she asked.

'What? What do you mean Alice?' I replied

I carried Alice into the hospital. After an injection, and a few kind words from the doctor, Alice's breathing was again under control. The doctor told us to take Alice home so that she could rest.

We were so happy. Phew! Alice was okay. She was going to be okay.

When all the tension of that evening started to leave us, it was only then that I was able to return to that question of Alice in the car.

'What happens next?'

Alice's fear, discomfort and pain in the car was very real but thanks to Mr. Twiddle she forgot these things. She was inside a story, and she was asking what happens next, that most human, that most magical of questions.

A story can do magic. Yes, indeed it can.

I finished Mr. Twiddle's story when I got home. Alice was very tired, but she didn't want to sleep until she knew what happened to poor Mr. Twiddle.

And so, his pyjama trousers fell down, he was chased by a dog, and he bought an alarm clock, and a new pair of pyjamas that very day.

We learnt later that Alice had an allergy to dust. We set to work and started cleaning the house. Alice's allergy cleared up and now it's something that we can laugh about when we look back.

Alice is now 24 years old. She is now a woman, but that little girl still lives inside her. She still reads stories. She still asks that magical question, 'what happens next'.

And I hope that you keep asking that question too, dear reader all of your life. It is a question that we should never stop asking at any age.

What happens next is the question that drives us to know more and to learn.

I hope that the stories you read will invite you to ask the question that Alice asked on that winter's day.

I put *Mr. Twiddle* back on the shelf, and smile to myself. That day Alice helped me to remember.

I remembered the power of the story, the magic. On that day, the little child in me came out again, wanting to know, 'what happens next?' Since that day this child is always by my side.

It was on this day that I decided that the thing I most wanted to do was to tell stories. It was on this day that I decided to become a writer. It was thanks to Alice's lesson that I wrote the story of Egghead. It is thanks to Alice that I am writing to you right now.

Thank you, all the children of the world. May we protect you for you are our precious future. And may we learn from you. And remember too.

Test Your Memory - Answers

1. Emee
2. Like the word, 'Bot'.
3. What happens next?
4. School years
5. The second industrial revolution
6. A Peach
7. Buuz
8. Because it's noisier and livelier.
9. She wanted a microscope because she is interested in the world of the small.
10. She listened at the living room door.
11. Madison is Boloroo's classmate. She calls Boloroo, 'science nerd'.
12. You can find happiness on the wings of a butterfly.
13. She examined some dust.
14. She saw her grandmother from Mongolia.
15. Boloroo's uncle.
16. To the cinema, the beach, Boloroo's school, shopping mall, zoo.
17. At the park

18 Happiness is right in front of your nose. All you have to do is smell the grass, look up at the sky or admire the wings of a butterfly. Enjoy the moment, now!

19 How much water do people use every day? Are there peaches in Mongolia? What's the most powerful microscope in the world? What do you have to do to become a history teacher? Has there been a third industrial revolution? Do dogs have feelings like us?

20 Tell others your answers to these questions! ☺

A Brief Preview of the next installment in the Boloroo series.

Coming soon in 2024.

Boloroo: The Next Adventure

Chapter 1 Across the Sky

Normally I don't like the sound of the alarm clock. But this morning it was different! I love the sound.

Beep! Beep! Beep! Beep!

This morning my alarm is not telling me that I have to go to school. No! It's a Saturday and I'm not going to school. The alarm is telling me that it's time to get up because my next adventure is going to begin.

Today I'm going on a journey.

But it's not just any journey. It's THE journey.

'Yes!' I shout.

My loud YES wakes my dog, Bankhar up and probably mum and dad too.

I get washed and dressed as quickly as I can and then I run down the corridor to mum and dad's bedroom. 'Mum, are you awake. We don't want to miss the plane. It's time to get up! Quickly!'

'We're awake,' says dad from the bedroom. 'And don't worry we've got lots of time. Our flight doesn't leave for another ten hours!

'Yes, dad. But we've got to take Bankhar to Olivia's house, before we leave for the airport.'

'Which will take ten minutes,' says dad.

'Okay! Maybe I am a little early. But it'll be so cool to get to the airport early and see all the other travellers and to try to understand where they are going to and what they are going to do. And we'll probably have a snack. And then we have to change our money because they don't accept euros where we are going. After this, we have to check in our suitcases before we go into the lounge area and we must not forget our passports and by the way have you packed everything? I made a list so that I know I have everything. It's important to remember to pack everything you need. Are you ready? It's a long journey and I can't wait and I am so excited.'

'Yes, we know,' says mum. 'We'll leave soon I promise. But let's have some breakfast first!'

There are so many people at the airport. And there is so much noise. Everybody is busy going somewhere. But where? Then I look up at the big departures board with all the exciting destinations. So many places!

'Look at all the places you can go, mum! I want to go to all of them.'

Madrid, Oslo, Boston, Athens, Frankfurt, Dublin, Warsaw, Paris, Stockholm, and then I saw it.

I saw our destination ………

Where is Boloroo going? Read part 2 of the Boloroo Story to find out.

Stories by Michael Lacey Freeman

Published Independently

Egghead the Movie (2023) A2 level

Boloroo's Big Question (2023) A2 level

Coming Soon:

The Drum – March 2024

Published with ELI Readers

Original Stories:

Egghead (2016) Winner Language Learner Literature Award A2 level

Dot to Dot (2018) A2 level

Adaptations of Classic Stories:

Anne of Green Gables (2013) LLL Award Winner A1 level

The Canterbury Tales (2014) LLL Award Winner A1 level

The Railway Children (2015) LLL Award Winner A1 level

Vanity Fair (2015) C1 level

The Portrait of a Lady (2016) B1 level

Black Beauty (2017) A1 level

The Thirty-Nine Steps (2017) A2 level

Mill on the Floss (2017) LLL Award Winner B2 level

Wind in the Willows (2019) A1 level

www.ingramcontent.com/pod-product-compliance
Lightning Source LLC
Chambersburg PA
CBHW070119110526
44587CB00015BA/2535